JUN 1 9

W9-AAZ-627

EARTH'S ENERGY EXPERIMENTS

WIND ENERGY
PROJECTS

Easy Energy Activities for
Future Engineers!

JESSIE ALKIRE

CONSULTING EDITOR, DIANE CRAIG, M.A./READING SPECIALIST

Super Sandcastle

An Imprint of Abdo Publishing
abdopublishing.com

DISCARDED
from Iowa City Public Library

IOWA CITY

JUN   2019

PUBLIC LIBRARY

abdopublishing.com

Published by Abdo Publishing, a division of ABDO, PO Box 398166, Minneapolis, Minnesota 55439. Copyright © 2019 by Abdo Consulting Group, Inc. International copyrights reserved in all countries. No part of this book may be reproduced in any form without written permission from the publisher. Super SandCastle™ is a trademark and logo of Abdo Publishing.

Printed in the United States of America, North Mankato, Minnesota
052018
092018

 THIS BOOK CONTAINS RECYCLED MATERIALS

Design and Production: Mighty Media, Inc.
Editor: Liz Salzmann
Cover Photographs: Mighty Media, Inc.; Shutterstock
Interior Photographs: iStockphoto; Mighty Media, Inc.; Shutterstock; Wikimedia Commons

The following manufacturers/names appearing in this book are trademarks: Artist's Loft™, Elmer's® Glue-All®, Sharpie®

Library of Congress Control Number: 2017961713

Publisher's Cataloging-in-Publication Data
Names: Alkire, Jessie, author.
Title: Wind energy projects: Easy energy activities for future engineers! / by Jessie Alkire.
Other titles: Easy energy activities for future engineers!
Description: Minneapolis, Minnesota : Abdo Publishing, 2019. | Series: Earth's energy experiments
Identifiers: ISBN 9781532115677 (lib.bdg.) | ISBN 9781532156397 (ebook)
Subjects: LCSH: Wind power--Juvenile literature. | Handicraft--Juvenile literature. | Science projects--Juvenile literature. | Air--Experiments--Juvenile literature.
Classification: DDC 333.92--dc23

Super SandCastle™ books are created by a team of professional educators, reading specialists, and content developers around five essential components—phonemic awareness, phonics, vocabulary, text comprehension, and fluency—to assist young readers as they develop reading skills and strategies and increase their general knowledge. All books are written, reviewed, and leveled for guided reading and early reading intervention programs for use in shared, guided, and independent reading and writing activities to support a balanced approach to literacy instruction.

TO ADULT HELPERS

The projects in this title are fun and simple. There are just a few things to remember to keep kids safe. Some projects require the use of sharp or hot objects. Also, kids may be using messy materials such as glue or paint. Make sure they protect their clothes and work surfaces. Review the projects before starting, and be ready to assist when necessary.

KEY SYMBOLS

Watch for these warning symbols in this book. Here is what they mean.

HOT!
You will be working with something hot. Get help!

SHARP!
You will be working with a sharp object. Get help!

CONTENTS

WHAT IS WIND ENERGY?

The air in Earth's atmosphere is constantly moving. This motion is wind. The force of wind creates energy. People use wind energy in different ways.

SAILBOAT RACE

People can use the wind directly. One way to use wind energy is to move sailboats. The harder the wind blows, the faster the boats go!

The wind can also be used indirectly. It turns wind turbines.

WINDMILLS IN THE NETHERLANDS

There are different kinds of wind turbines. Some do **mechanical** work, such as pumping water or grinding grains. These are often called windmills.

Other wind turbines turn **generators**. These create electricity. This method of producing electricity is popular because it does not create pollution. Wind energy is also renewable. This means we cannot use it up.

WIND TURBINES THAT CREATE ELECTRICITY

HOW WE USE WIND ENERGY

Today, wind energy is mainly used for electricity. This electricity is used to power homes, water systems, and more.

TURBINES

Turbines convert wind energy into electricity. A wind turbine usually has three blades. The blades are on a tower that is more than 100 feet (31 m) tall! Turbines are often grouped together. This is called a wind farm.

HOW TURBINES WORK

Wind causes a turbine's blades to spin. The blades are connected to a **rotor** and shaft. The rotor and shaft turn with the blades. The shaft has gears that turn a **generator**. This produces electricity. A **transformer** increases the strength of the electricity. Then the electricity travels through power lines to homes and businesses.

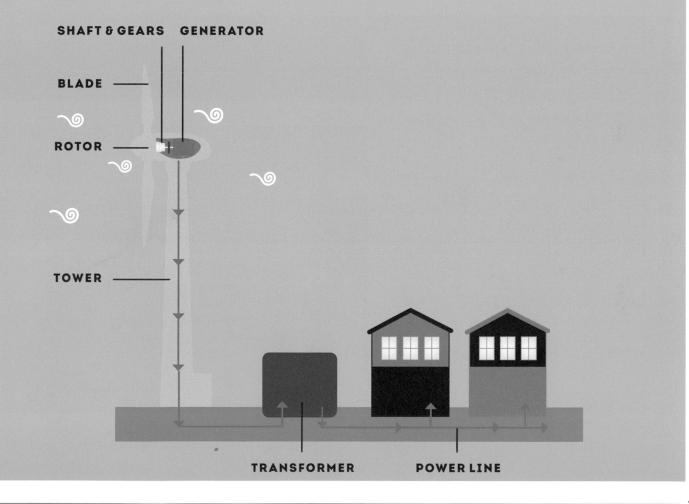

SHAFT & GEARS   GENERATOR

BLADE

ROTOR

TOWER

TRANSFORMER   POWER LINE

WIND ENERGY HISTORY

Wind energy has been used for more than seven thousand years. Its earliest use was to move sailboats. Sailing is still a popular type of boating.

People started building windmills more than one thousand years ago. The first windmills were in an area that is now part of Iran. They pumped water and ground grains. The use of windmills quickly spread across the world. Many are still in use today.

WINDMILL IN NEBRASKA

CHARLES F. BRUSH

Charles F. Brush was an American inventor. He lived in Ohio. Brush worked with light and electricity. In 1888, Brush built the first **automatic** wind turbine. It was 60 feet (18 m) tall. It had 144 blades! The turbine charged batteries in Brush's basement. The batteries powered electric lights throughout the house.

OFFSHORE WIND FARM

In the 1800s, people began building wind turbines to create electricity. Since then, wind turbines have continued to be improved.

Today, large wind farms are being built around the world. There are even wind farms in the ocean! Scientists believe that wind energy will continue to provide more of the world's power!

MATERIALS

Here are some of the materials that you will need for the projects in this book.

BOTTLE CAPS

CARD STOCK

CRAFT GLUE

CRAFT KNIFE

DC MOTOR (12V)

DUCT TAPE

ELECTRICAL TAPE

**HEAVY-DUTY
SMALL HOLE
PUNCH**

HOLE PUNCH

**HOT GLUE GUN
& GLUE STICKS**

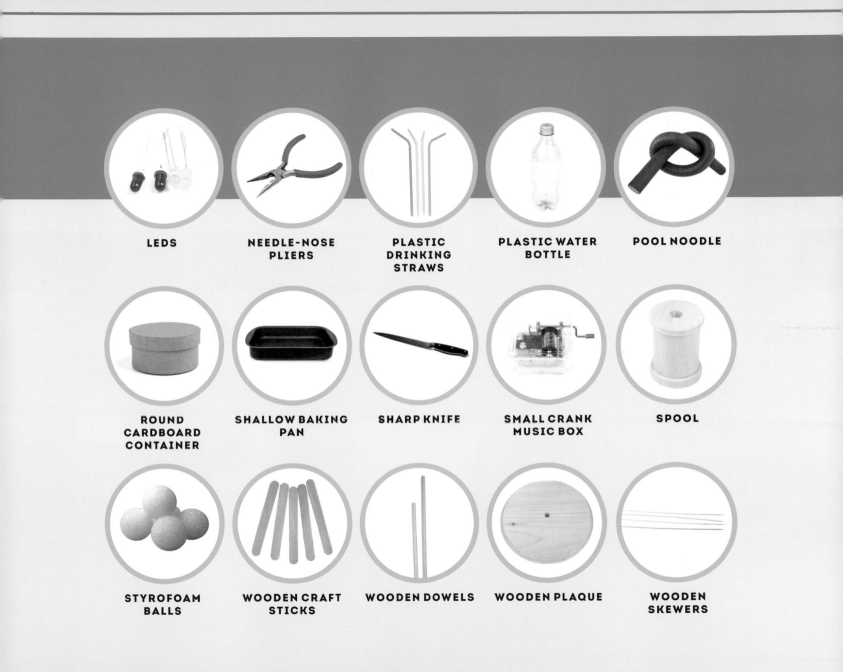

LEDS

NEEDLE-NOSE
PLIERS

PLASTIC
DRINKING
STRAWS

PLASTIC WATER
BOTTLE

POOL NOODLE

ROUND
CARDBOARD
CONTAINER

SHALLOW BAKING
PAN

SHARP KNIFE

SMALL CRANK
MUSIC BOX

SPOOL

STYROFOAM
BALLS

WOODEN CRAFT
STICKS

WOODEN DOWELS

WOODEN PLAQUE

WOODEN
SKEWERS

POOL NOODLE SAILBOATS

MATERIALS: pool noodle, sharp knife, ruler, pencil, card stock, scissors, wooden craft sticks, craft glue, clear tape, shallow baking pan, water

Sailboats use wind to move. The wind pushes on the sail. This causes the boat to move across the water.

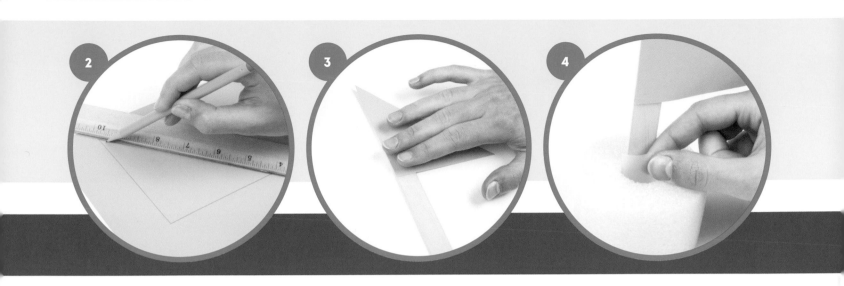

① Have an adult help you cut a 2-inch (5 cm) piece off of the pool noodle. This is the hull of your boat.

② Draw a triangle on the card stock. Make sure the triangle has a right angle. Cut out the triangle. This is your sail.

③ Put glue along one of the shorter edges of the sail. Press it to a wooden craft stick with a corner at one end of the stick.

④ Push the other end of the craft stick into the center of the pool noodle piece. Tape the craft stick in place.

⑤ Repeat steps 1 through 4 to make more boats.

⑥ Pour about 1 inch (2.5 cm) of water into the baking pan.

⑦ Place your boats in the pan. Use wind to move your boats. Blow on them, wave a magazine, or take the pan outside on a windy day.

BALLOON CAR

MATERIALS: 3 plastic drinking straws, scissors, plastic water bottle, wooden skewer, clear tape, 4 bottle caps, hammer, nail, scrap wood, hot glue gun & glue sticks, craft knife, balloon

Wind is moving air. This motion has **kinetic energy**. Kinetic energy can be used to **propel** a balloon car.

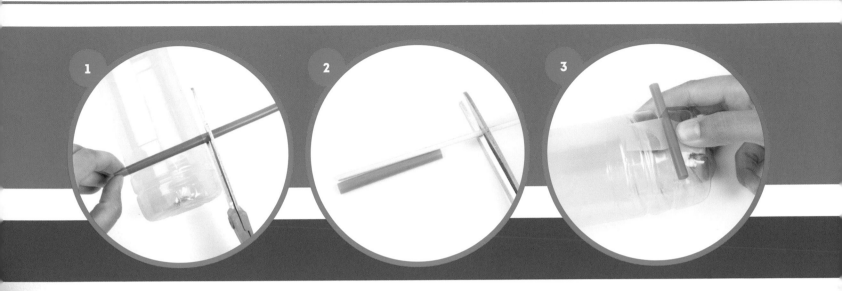

1 Cut two pieces off of a drinking straw. These pieces should be as long as the bottle is wide.

2 Cut two pieces off of a wooden skewer. These should be a little longer than the straw pieces.

3 Tape one straw piece across the side of the bottle near the bottom.

4 Tape the other straw piece slightly below the curve of the top of the bottle. Make sure the two straw pieces are **parallel**.

Continued on the next page.

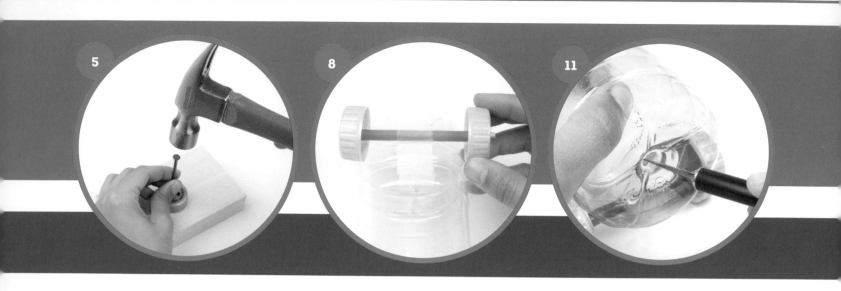

5 Place a bottle cap on a piece of scrap wood. Have an adult help you use a hammer and nail to make a hole in the center of the cap.

6 Repeat step 5 with the other bottle caps.

7 Stick one end of a skewer piece into the hole in a bottle cap.

8 Slide the skewer into one of the straw pieces. Stick the other end of the skewer into the hole in another bottle cap.

9 Repeat steps 7 and 8 with the other skewer piece, bottle caps, and straw piece. These are the car's wheels.

10 Add hot glue to secure the wheels to the skewers if necessary.

11 Have an adult help you use a craft knife to cut an X into the bottom of the bottle.

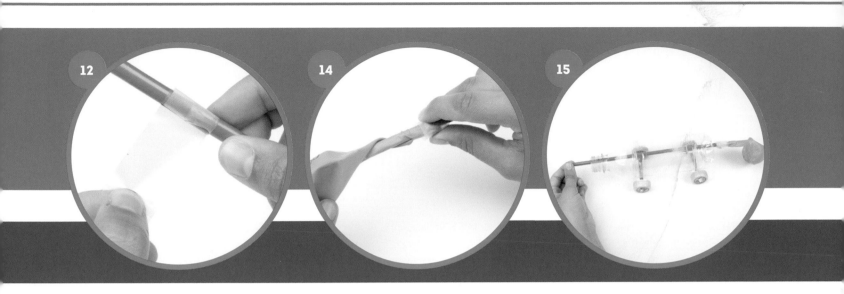

12 Tape two straws together to make a straw that is longer than the bottle is tall.

13 Put the balloon over one end of the straw. Pinch the balloon to make sure there isn't any air inside it.

14 Wrap tape around the neck of the balloon and the straw. Make sure the balloon is tightly sealed.

15 Push the straw through the X in the bottle. The end of the straw should stick out of the top of the bottle.

16 Blow into the straw to put air in the balloon. Pinch the end of the straw so the air doesn't come out.

17 Set the car on a flat, smooth surface. Let go of the straw and watch your car move!

LIFTING CHALLENGE

MATERIALS: newspaper, milk or juice carton, paint, paintbrush, water, 2 wooden skewers, Styrofoam ball, hot glue gun & glue sticks, card stock, pencil, scissors, tape, spool, string, paper cup, marbles or other weights, fan (optional)

Windmills turn wind energy into **mechanical** energy. This energy can be used to lift heavy objects! How much can your model windmill lift?

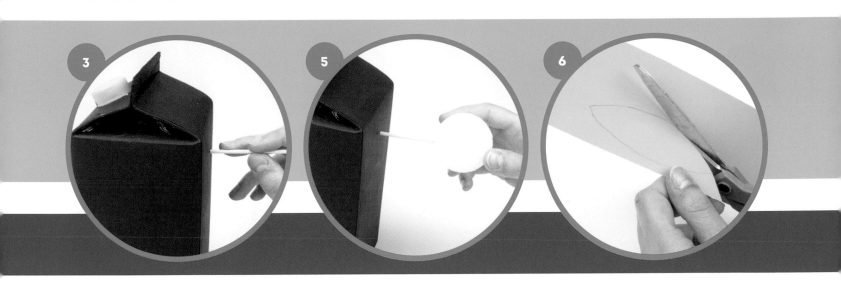

① Cover your work surface with newspaper. Paint the carton. Let the paint dry.

② Fill the carton about one-fourth full with water. Close the cap tightly.

③ Poke a wooden skewer through the carton near the top.

④ Push the skewer through the carton so it makes holes on both sides. Wiggle the skewer to make the holes a little bigger.

⑤ Stick a Styrofoam ball on one end of the skewer. Remove the ball. Put hot glue inside the hole. Stick the ball back on the skewer.

⑥ Draw three windmill blade shapes on card stock. Cut them out.

⑦ Cut the other wooden skewer into three equal pieces.

Continued on the next page.

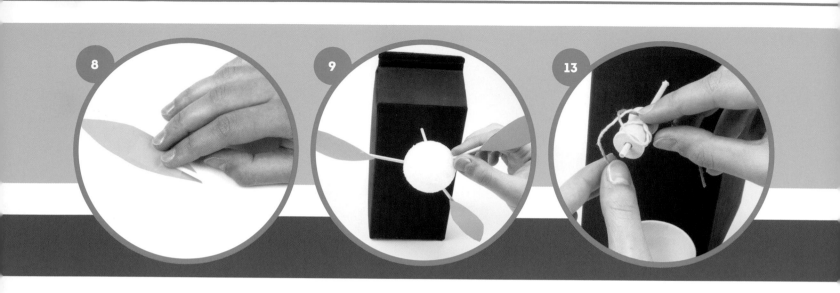

8 Tape a blade to one end of each short skewer.

9 Push the short skewers into the foam ball. Space them evenly. The short skewers should be **perpendicular** to the long skewer.

10 Put hot glue inside the spool. Slide the spool onto the other end of the long skewer.

11 Cut a long piece of string. Make it at least as long as the carton is tall.

12 Tape one end of the string inside a paper cup.

13 Tie the other end of the string to the spool. Knot the string a few times so it is secure.

14 Place your windmill outside on a windy day or put it in front of a fan.

15 Set the cup under the spool. Put marbles, rocks, or other weights in the cup.

16 Observe your windmill as it spins. Can it lift the cup? Try removing some weight or adding more.

DIGGING DEEPER

The windmill in this project works a lot like a windmill that grinds grain. They both use wind energy to turn a shaft. But the shaft of a grain mill has gears that turn millstones inside the mill. Millstones are large stones that lie one on top of the other. The top stone remains still. The bottom stone turns. The grain is ground up between the stones.

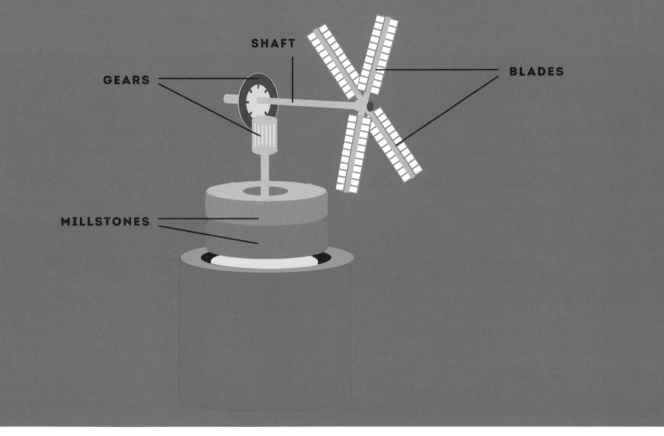

SHAFT

BLADES

GEARS

MILLSTONES

WIND MUSIC BOX

MATERIALS: newspaper, 2 wooden dowels, wooden plaque, paint, paintbrush, hot glue gun & glue sticks, bowl that is about 5 inches (12 cm) across, card stock, pen, scissors, hole punch, small crank music box, beads (optional), fan (optional)

Anemometers measure wind speed. These devices use cups that spin around when the wind blows into them. You can build an anemometer to power a music box!

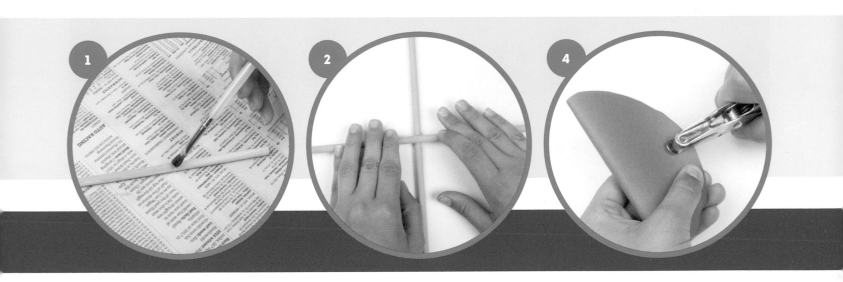

1 Cover your work surface with newspaper. Paint the dowels and wooden plaque. Let the paint dry.

2 Hot glue the centers of the dowels together to form a cross shape. Hold the dowels in place until the glue dries.

3 Trace the bowl four times on card stock. Cut out the circles.

4 Bend a card stock circle in half but don't flatten the fold. Punch a hole near the edge where the sides meet.

5 Repeat step 4 to punch holes in the other three circles.

Continued on the next page.

6 Glue the music box to the center of the wooden plaque. Make sure the **crank** points up.

7 The crank has a handle that spins around on the shaft. Cover the handle and shaft with hot glue so the handle can't spin.

8 Put a large dot of hot glue on the dowels where they cross.

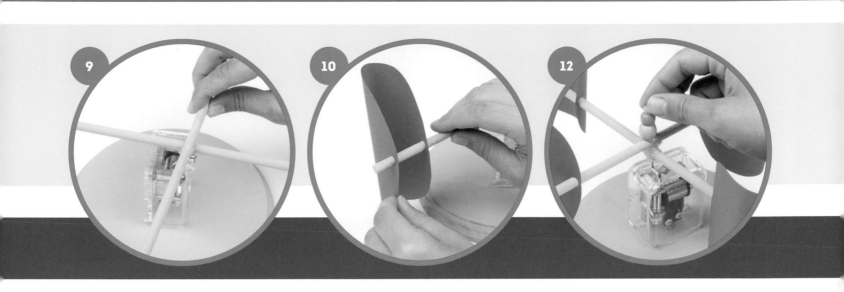

⑨ Turn the dowels over and press the glue onto the **crank**. Hold the dowels in place until the glue dries.

⑩ Push the end of a dowel through both holes of a card stock circle. The circle should be slightly bent.

⑪ Repeat step 10 to put the other circles on the other ends of the dowels. Make sure the bend in each circle points to the right.

⑫ Glue beads or other decorations to the crossed dowels.

⑬ Bring your music box **anemometer** outside on a windy day or put it in front of a fan. Listen to the wind play music!

TERRIFIC TURBINE GENERATOR

MATERIALS: small paper cup, scissors, 2 wooden craft sticks, ruler, marker, heavy-duty small hole punch, 12V DC motor, hot glue gun & glue sticks, needle-nose pliers, LED, electrical tape, round cardboard container with lid, duct tape, fan (optional)

Most wind energy today is used for electricity. This electricity is produced using wind turbines. Try making a model turbine that can power an LED bulb!

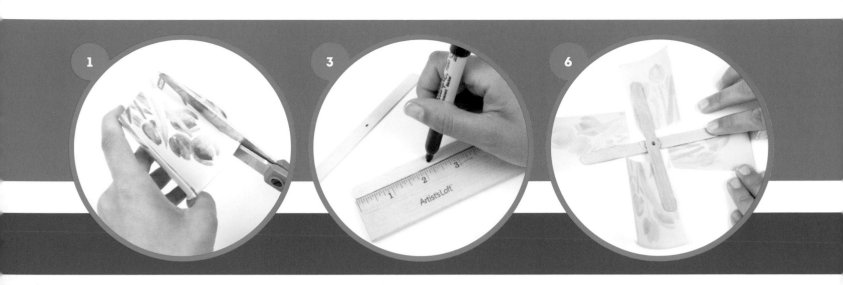

1. Make four cuts from the top to the bottom of the cup. Space them evenly.

2. Cut around the bottom of the cup to separate the side pieces. These are the turbine's blades.

3. Make a mark in the center of each craft stick.

4. Use a heavy-duty small hole punch to make a hole at each mark. Make sure the hole is large enough for the motor's shaft to fit inside.

5. Hot glue the centers of the craft sticks together to form a cross shape. Make sure the holes don't get covered with glue.

6. Hot glue the edge of a blade to the end of each craft stick.

Continued on the next page.

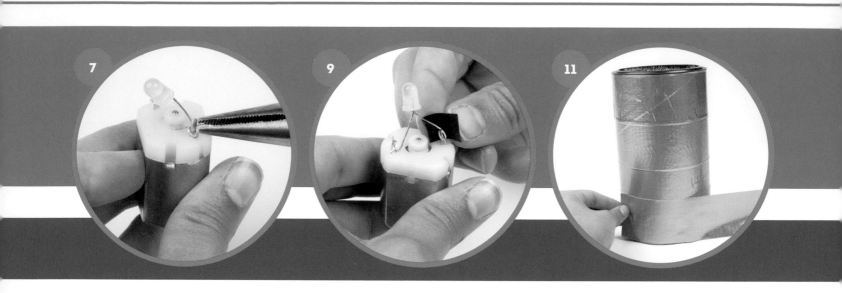

7 Use the pliers to twist one of the LED's leads around each metal connection point on the back of the motor.

8 Test the connection by turning the motor's shaft with your fingers. If the LED doesn't light up, try switching the leads.

9 Wrap the wires and connection points with electrical tape.

10 Put the lid on the container.

11 Cover the container and lid with decorative duct tape.

Wind energy is often used to power lights. Some people have small turbines at their homes. These small turbines work just like larger turbines. They can power lights directly. Or, the power can be stored for later use!

12 Hot glue the motor to the edge of the container. Make sure the shaft sticks out past the edge.

13 Add the blades by sliding the hole in the craft sticks over the motor's shaft. Hot glue the craft sticks to the shaft.

14 Bring your turbine outside on a windy day or put it in front of a fan.

15 Observe the turbine as it spins. Does it create enough energy to turn on the LED?

CONCLUSION

Wind is a growing energy **resource** today. It is clean and renewable. Wind turbines create electricity. Scientists are working to make turbines work even better!

QUIZ

1. The air in Earth's atmosphere never moves. **TRUE OR FALSE?**

2. What is a group of wind turbines called?

3. When was the first **automatic** wind turbine invented?

LEARN MORE ABOUT IT!

You can find out more about wind energy at the library. Or you can ask an adult to help you **research** wind energy on the internet!

Answers: 1. False   2. Wind farm   3. 1888

GLOSSARY

anemometer – an instrument for measuring the speed of the wind.

automatic – moving or acting by itself.

crank – a handle that is turned to start or run a machine.

generator – a machine that creates electricity.

kinetic energy – energy associated with motion.

mechanical – made or operated by a machine or a tool.

parallel – lying or moving in the same direction but always the same distance apart.

perpendicular – going straight up or to the side at a 90-degree angle from another line or surface.

propel – to cause to move forward.

research – to find out more about something.

resource – something that is usable or valuable.

rotor – a machine part that spins around another part.

transformer – a device that changes the voltage of an electric current.